PLEASE

JANINE AMOS

Published in the United States by Windmill Books (Alphabet Soup)
Windmill Books
303 Park Avenue South
Suite #1280
New York, NY 10010-3657

U.S. publication copyright ©Evans Brothers Limited 2009
First North American Edition

Library of Congress Cataloging-in-Publication Data

Amos, Janine
      Please / Janine Amos.
          p.   cm. – (Best behavior)
      Contents: Monty's ball—Harry's juice—A story for Lilly.
      Summary: Three brief stories demonstrate the importance of being polite and
using "Please" when asking for help.
      ISBN 978-1-60754-023-6 (lib.) – 978-1-60754-038-0 (pbk.)
978-1-60754-039-7 (6 pack)
      1. Courtesy—Juvenile literature   2. Conduct of life—Juvenile literature
[1. Etiquette   2. Conduct of life]   I. Title   II. Series
      395.1'22—dc22

American Library Binding 13-digit ISBN: 978-1-60754-023-6
Paperback 13-digit ISBN: 978-1-60754-038-0
6 pack 13-Digit ISBN: 978-1-60754-039-7

Manufactured in China

Credits:
Editor: Louise John
Designer: Mark Holt
Photography: Gareth Boden
Production: Jenny Mulvanney

With thanks to:
Genna and Karen Heron, Harry Foster, Montel Adams, and Gareth, Annie, Lilly, and Murray Boden.

Monty's Ball

Murray kicks the ball.

4

It goes into Mr. Boden's garden.

Please may I have the ball?

Murray asks for the ball back.

6

Mr. Boden throws it back.

Give me the ball!

8

Next time Monty asks for the ball.

Why does Mr. Boden say No?

No, I won't.

9

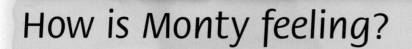

How is Monty feeling?

How is Mr. Boden feeling?

Please may I have the ball back?

12

Monty tries again.

How does Mr. Boden feel now?

Harry's Juice

Get me the juice.

16

Harry can't reach the juice.
Genna can.

Why won't Genna help Harry?
How does she feel?

18

Harry thinks about it.
What could he do?

He tries again.

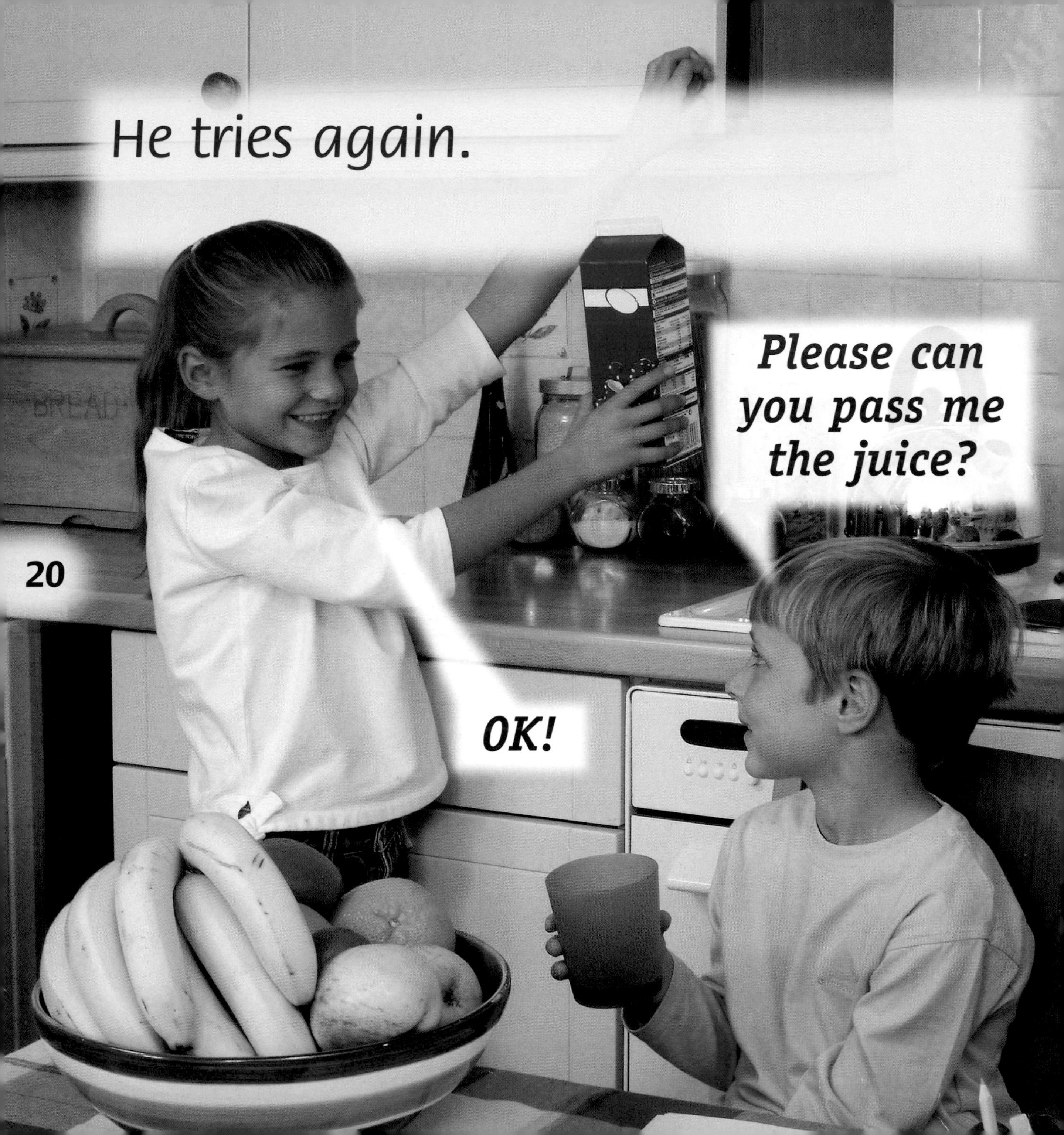

A Story for Lilly

Lilly is tired.

I want another story.

But so is her mom.

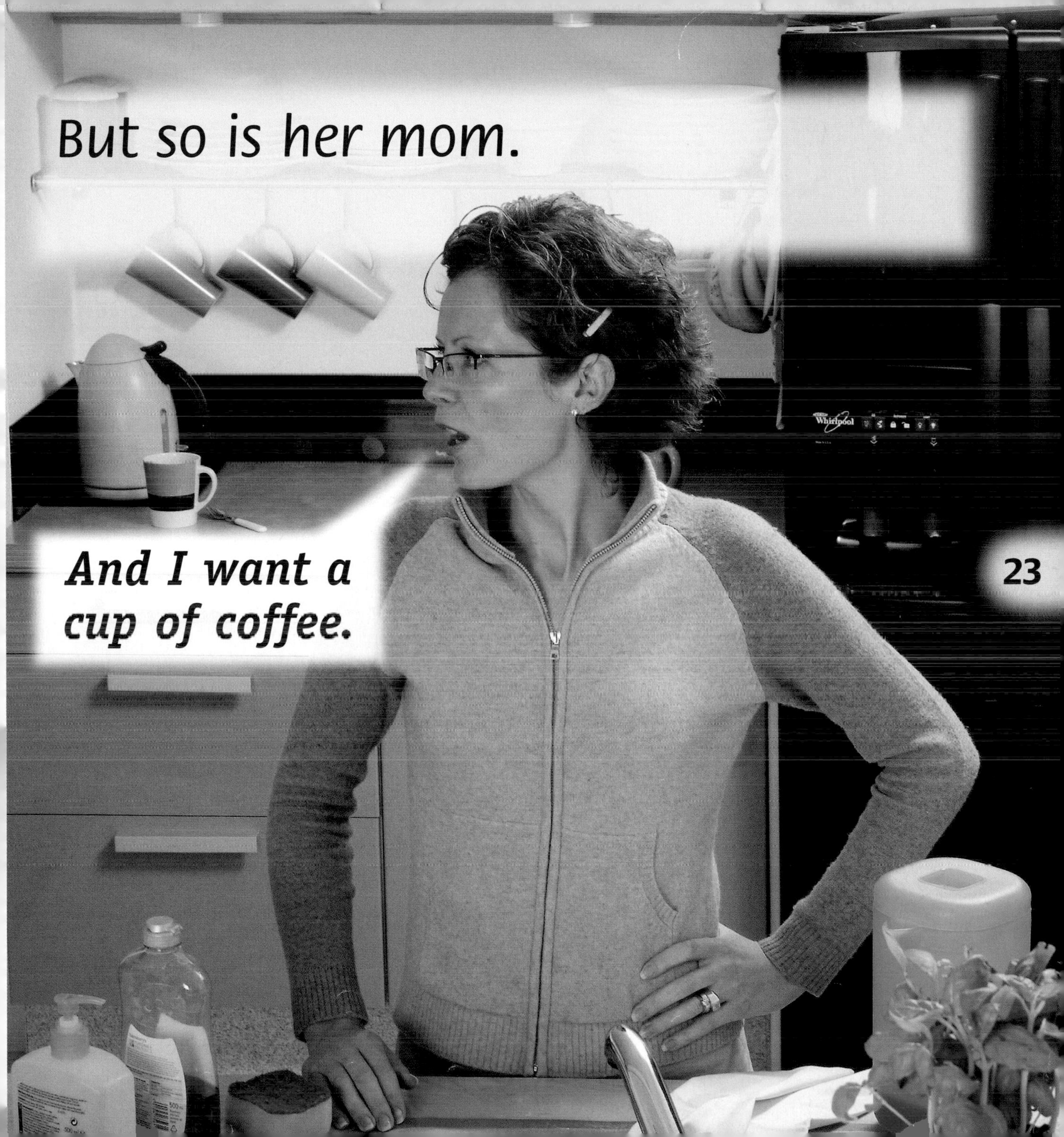

Lilly tries again.
So does her mom.

24

Please may I
have a story?

Please wait until I have made my coffee.

How does Lilly feel?
How does her mom feel?

Lilly looks at her book and waits.

Mom drinks her coffee.

Then she reads Lilly a story.

Most people are glad to help if they are asked.

But they don't like being told what to do.

30

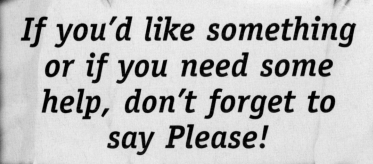

And sometimes you'll need to wait until they are ready.

31

If you'd like something or if you need some help, don't forget to say Please!

FOR FURTHER READING

INFORMATION BOOKS

Carlson, Nancy. *How to Lose all Your Friends*. New York: Puffin, 1997.

Verdick, Elizabeth. *Words Are Not For Hurting*. Minneapolis: Free Spirit, 2004.

FICTION

Keller, Laurie. *Do Unto Otters: A Book About Manners*. New York: Henry Holt & Co., 2007.

Morris, Jennifer. *May I Please Have a Cookie? (Scholastic Reader)*. New York: Cartwheel Books, 2005.

AUTHOR BIO
Janine has worked in publishing as an editor and author, as a lecturer in education. Her interests are in personal growth and raising self-esteem and she works with educators, child psychologists and specialists in mediation. She has written more than fifty books for children. Many of her titles deal with first time experiences and emotional health issues such as Bullying, Death, and Divorce.

You can find more great fiction and nonfiction from Windmill Books at windmillbks.com